Open Between Us

Open Between Us

Poems by George Looney

Turning Point

Published by Turning Point
P.O. Box 541106
Cincinnati, OH 45254-1106

ISBN: 9781934999981
LCCN: 2010929005

Poetry Editor: Kevin Walzer
Business Editor: Lori Jareo

Visit us on the web at www.turningpointbooks.com

The poems in this book first appeared in the following journals, often in earlier versions.

Poetry East: "How It All Is" (as "Letter to Smith From Chicago") and "For the Workers of Machinists Union, Local 765." *Poets On: Forgetting:* "The Hurt World Worth Having." *Mississippi Valley Review:* "Of Light and Moisture" (as "Of Light, Moisture, and the Census of Birds"). *The Literary Review:* "Breaking the Surface," "The Worst We Can Do," and "Local Anesthesia." *The Kenyon Review:* "No Matter the Weather." *Tar River Poetry:* "Into the River You Lost" (as "A Geography of the Ohio"), "A Space so Filled With Grief" (as "A Small Space so Filled With Grief"), "White Explosions," and "Acceptable Damage." *Southern Poetry Review:* "Irrefutable Evidence." *Cold Mountain Review:* "House on Poplar Street" and "What Brings Us to Ourselves." *Black Warrior Review:* "Learning to Name the Water" (as "Songs I Know by Heart and Love") and "Carbon Cycle." *Poets On: Escaping:* "Testament." *Poets On: Healing:* "In the Stunned Body." *Indiana Review:* "Birds." *Sulphur River Literary Review:* "An Egret in Flight" and "The Weight of a Foot on Grass" (as "The Art of Needing"). *The Texas Review:* "Weightless" (as "Release") and "One Form Love Takes." *Cincinnati Poetry Review:* "How Breath Escapes Us" (as "Diving Cold Into This Life"). *Puerto Del Sol:* "The Reassurance of Soil." *River Wind:* "Renditions of Men." *Cimarron Review:* "The Unspeakable" (as "Threatening Light") and "With Bread to Fill the Air." *Mississippi Review:* "Navigation Without Numbers." *Permafrost:* "A Sad Ballad Haunted by Coffee" (as "Dark on Its Own"). *Oxford Magazine:* "Fallen from Grace" and "Storms We Can't Name." *Prairie Schooner:* "Acts of Erasure and Acceptance" (as "Acts of Erasure, Acts of Acceptance"). *The Gettysburg Review:* "Trusting Your Way Home." *Cottonwood:* "Open Between Us."

"Breaking the Surface" won the Charles Angoff Award from *The Literary Review*, and was reprinted in *Editor's Choice III*.

For Mairi and for Douglas

Table of Contents

How It All Is 11
The Hurt World Worth Having 13
Of Light and Moisture 16
Breaking the Surface 18
No Matter the Weather 20
Into the River You Lost 22
A Space so Filled With Grief 24
Irrefutable Evidence 26
House on Poplar Street 28
Learning to Name the Water 31
Testament 33
In the Stunned Body 35
Birds 37
An Egret in Flight 39
Weightless 41
The Weight of a Foot on Grass 42
Carbon Cycle 44
For the Workers of Machinists' Union, Local 765 46
How Breath Escapes Us 49
One Form Love Takes 51
The Reassurance of Soil 53
Renditions of Men 55
The Unspeakable 56
Navigation Without Numbers 58
A Sad Ballad Haunted by Coffee 61
The Worst We Can Do 63
White Explosions 65
Fallen from Grace 67
What Brings Us to Ourselves 69
Storms We Can't Name 71
With Bread to Fill the Air 72
Acceptable Damage 74
Acts of Erasure and Acceptance 76
Local Anesthesia 79
Trusting Your Way Home 81
Open Between Us 84

So the land is wrong and it is empty
—Lucia Perillo

How It All Is

Voices from the street are gone
before I can respond.

The drunk who yelled what he thought
was love to a woman
who called the police to haul him off.

Or the madness of this wind shivering
clouds between buildings
and over grass in a city park

where children run laughing through fog
as though it were there for them,

not fallen over everything to become
an image in a poem
with no clear idea except how human it all is.

A woman practices the cello
across the courtyard. Sometimes
at night I watch her feed her cat.

It's a comfort to know something,
at least, is well cared for.

~

The man whose voice taught me
what it's like to love
so much the world has to be a witness,

I want him to come back and be
let in, despite being
drunk, hope a bruised woman.

How predictable this sore world can be.
Always take as much of it in
as you can, my friend, to love.

The Hurt World Worth Having

The old couple upstairs needs things
sedate, their bodies
scarred by past disturbances.

Anything could stop their hearts,
even my son crying
to be fed. Their bodies

fragile, they've lost touch
with the grammar
of human company. They watch

the news, only the weather
real, the rest
a barrage of sentences

for others. They remember
weather can erase
things. Survivors live with

scars. Where my wife was opened
to lift our son out,
the requisite scar remains.

~

Outside, everything not tied down
is moving. No telling
where this wind will stop.

It might break across the graveyard
at the end of this street
and wake the dead who return

to fit into the familiar
wounds and love
the pain they know will be

temporary. A town broken
by weather is
on the news. Rescuers get sick

over bodies caught off guard
by wind, and loss
drifts off the rubble left behind

by what's already playing Bach
on my windows. I want
to keep this wind from the bodies

I love. My wife's scar
catches stray light
in the dark, glows. Grief

can scar flesh with memory,
but this isn't sorrow.
When we open our bodies

~

to deny loss, our scars
remind us
what we weather in order

to translate the loss
flesh inherits
into a livable calm.

Of Light and Moisture

Gulls cross in flight. I'd love to
dive up and break the surface
of this air. Everything's wet,

erosion something we live with.
After showering, I dry
your body with tenderness and cloth

that responds to the needs of
our flesh. Gulls cry at
being left to circle above pain and relief,

angels breaking through the sky
from the other side. How close
they come to touching. This

light bruises the places we live
and our bodies. Of light,
moisture, and a census of birds,

I'd forge a history of loss. The world
refuses to have anything
to do with our grief, though gulls

~

harangue the sky, harridan ghosts
whose voices echo the urge
of our grounded bodies to rise.

Breaking the Surface

Loss, just the threat of it, drives us
to a nearby town with a bar
open another hour. In the parking lot,

the fins of old cars remind me
of monsters I believe
still break the calm of certain bodies

of water. Over gin we discuss
Lacan's Other, its relation
to children pulled from the Ohio

Wright elegized. Both of us believe
the Other's who we speak of
when we speak of things breaking

the surface, that the Other is
our disgust of ourselves
taking form. We rage against

how it creates legends. We'd like to
drop depth charges, leave it
for dead. All we can do is keep watch

~

and note the risings. Come this far
for gin, we hope to make it back
without loss. In Scotland, people gather

at Loch Ness with cameras to
capture what they believe in.
We believe what rises from any murk

is what we let loose. That it returns
to remind us words are born of loss
and to take us home when the last bar

open anywhere closes and the gin and talk
come to nothing—the way back
a dark state route where lovers pull off

and park in fields. All the way home
we know what's happening,
fins breaking the surface of winter wheat.

No Matter the Weather

Ice claims the world with light it reflects
shed by the rooms we gather in.

Surrounded by others, denied what makes us
who we are, the way we touch
and breathe, the pale slope of your naked back,

we leave to follow an owl you say is ours
to the river. How far the other side is.
As far as anything desired. After

we cross back over the cold that could have
carried us off, our guests go home.
Gathering up glasses, we laugh at the risk

we wouldn't have mentioned on the ice.
Outside, our breath
would rise, a signal of relief. Later,

as you sleep, I think of how we left our party
to walk through a world
assuming forms the cold insists on.

Even at this hour, someone too poor
to own a shanty
has made a hole in the ice, his line drifting

~

into a world where things live and die
without need of his imagination, or mine.

Deep enough, the cold remains a rumor.
The forecast of more snow
won't keep him from catching what he can.

Just as no fear keeps us from touching
in the ways we know. There is always a risk
of falling in. Your breath

comforts me with its cadence, my body
fit to yours. Nearby,

under snow-dusted ice, something's caught
sharp on what had seemed harmless.

Into the River You Lost

for James Wright

It was pain that moved you to speak of the river
and the heart that can lurk so long in the body

and yet blossom given the chance. The river was
a purgatory that could be
redeemed around any bend.

Maybe those the hook found could forgive you
in some way you never felt forgiven.

Maybe their broken bodies could forgive
a dying river
under a sky you might have said

was a longing for home, for the simple geography
of the Ohio I knew as distant coal barges

adrift under bridges. A river broken by cement.
I got close enough only once
to know it the way you did.

A friend and I, drinking, had come to
watch the barge lights.
Our empty cans, in the black water,

~

caught the distant lights and seemed to rise.
My friend said they looked like angels
and stepped into the river

you lost so much to, laughing, saying names
he learned in church. The dead you loved

with common words forgave his foolish effort
to clean up this world. He made it back,

sobered by his surviving. Tonight, you wait
by a river for Annie, sure she'll come.

In sycamores near the water cicadas sing.
You would join in
with a folk tune or one of the old hymns

you learned as a boy. Far from our Ohio,
your words make me believe

we can survive any darkness, as long
as we forgive the dead,
who forgive us. As long as we can

touch our bodies to the river and rise,
singing or naming what could be angels.

A Space so Filled With Grief

for June Sylvester

You'd become famous for
exposing your backside.
Mooning, it's called.

But the moon's as dark as anything
we could conjure.
It relies on another's light. You always said

we had no choice but to do the same.
I should have told you how I had
been mistaken for a doctor,

having brought a friend to the ER.
A woman held her burned son out to me,
but I couldn't bring back the dead.

You'd have wanted to be in this elegy.
To step out into the sad rain
igniting the light. Pale, shimmering woman,

you'd have ignored the rain to hold
the trembling body burning
in the storm-light—a man, suddenly

~

father to a ghost, who couldn't enter
any space so filled with grief.
The moon, it rises every night. Tonight,

risen orange, light it offers the water
and buildings and bodies
out walking is beautiful enough

to make the world into something
that could bless even
your damaged body, even mine.

Irrefutable Evidence

In Wahrheit singen, ist ein andrer Hauch.
Ein Hauch um nichts. Ein Wehn im Gott. Ein Wind.
—Rilke

A ruined mattress drops to the dirt
in the courtyard. Yesterday,
a man's voice rose from the dead

and dying grass to plead with the woman
he loved who called the police.
Risen from sleep, my wife and I listened,

as lost as Orpheus who, unnerved
by trembling shades, began
to wonder why he ever thought

music could continue after the ears
are gray flesh. He needed
to believe everything alive sings

and believes in song. Even the man
led off screaming his love
to a woman past believing him.

Orpheus was right. Even now,
the mattress trembles with a bruised music,
irrefutable evidence of the violence

~

in our lives. The music of loss.
When he needed to touch
his wife to believe, Orpheus lost

everything. Fearing the same fate,
I touch my wife, asleep.
Her body blesses me. Remaining.

House on Poplar Street

All forms that perish other forms supply.
—Alexander Pope

Patterns

The interstate came through and buried it.
Faith was easier, living in one place.
There are photographs of the house

where I learned things struggle to remain,
ghostly buds blooming on the near-dead oak
whose gnarled roots broke the backyard

where I buried pets I haven't thought of
for years. All of us seek the comfort
of talking to the dead in some form.

Carvings on rock and bone whisper
in glass cases in museums
everywhere. Place is its own history.

I'd have to carve runes into the road
to be clarified by headlights.
This used to be open land. The corpses

of animals mark off the distances,
the long patterns of living
hard to break. Memories lead back to

~

actual places. The ache of what's not
left forces these lines into
a form where ghosts come to rest.

Belief

Surfaces I knew by touch are missing.
In landscapes where ghosts
say words that comforted them

alive, I pass ruins and count the miles,
saying the names of towns
where it's possible to find more

than the lonely figure of the local spire.
The faith that keeps people fixing
what breaks can be found in towns

named by dull white signs. What I broke
in the house on Poplar Street
can't be fixed, and though I want

to believe in the names I carved
with butter knives
in painted wood, belief isn't enough.

This elegy can't summon back anything
that could ever speak.
What we touch of what we love is mute.

Names

Form is the passion for return, but this
can only come back
to a place no longer real,

where an oak stood that continued,
in the death cracking its heart,
to feed pale blooms that broke each year

from its scarred limbs. This was faith,
the struggle to keep providing.
Ghosts that wander between towns

with words they've loved can name
the places they are forgetting.
From us they want the names of

what we've touched. I want what I know
to be enough to satisfy the ghosts
who speak names they can't

bear to forget, like *poplar*. I want to be
able to pass on through them,
the familiar all I need to sustain me.

Learning to Name the Water

The strange water, the
Ohio river, that is no tomb to
Rise from the dead
From.
—James Wright

This river reflects human structures and desires
to carve its own niche,

carrying stories that go back to the first tribe
that chanted its name—Ohio.

I want to come home to this river
where the barges mark off distances,
to lie down in thick grass by this water

that would hold me in its depths and sing me
to sleep with hymns of familiar breath,
flooding my salty heart with its music.

Fishermen lower lines into the fish-stink,
boats rocking one spot as if persistence

were the only virtue in a world
where lines drift, disguised,
taken to sudden dances of deception and loss.

~

Old men simmer in the watery sun and dream.
Boats go out, draped with nets.
Barges drift by, coal, black and furious,

locked in holds. Fishermen wave to
the men smudged by coal smoke,
waiting for the lines to go taut. Music

marks off our lives. Drinking in a bar,
a juke box playing song after song,
one calls back some pleasure we had

thought lost. Like the night you and I
went down to the river
to watch the distant, slow-moving lights.

You danced to a faint, tinny music
for the dim outlines of men
stuck working nights on the barges.

What is this desire to claim we shared
a history on a river miles to the east?
Is fiction a salve we slap on our past?

Tonight, leaning over to kiss you
while you sleep, murmuring,
I can't understand anything other

than going on, as long as lights dance
like music on any dark, moving water.

Testament

The weathered white sign warns not to stop.
Prison Area, it says. Everyone's

nervous. What was your crime? I want
to ask the stranger beside me.

A storm moves in, the change in light
something I want to remember,
shadows slipping over eroded land.

Her hand touches my thigh. Someone coughs.
The sound seems to break the world.

Her hand on my thigh is warm.
Warm enough, I hope,
to hold as things go dark with the storm.

Another woman wakes. *Where are you?*
When will you be home? she asks,
then stops, realizing where she is.

The woman beside me is asleep,
the landscape broken by rain.

~

I won't tell her how the storm, the bus,
even her warm breath on my arm
are witnesses. How everything is

called to testify, to take the stand and swear
on the blackest of books.

A watery light alters this landscape
that leads to another nameless place

where I hope to sleep in the arms of someone
who can hold me as if it matters.

In the Stunned Body

We are older than our scars.
—Richard Hugo

Though he was talking of drink,
we know how much more
Hugo meant, our wounds

more obvious than those it takes years
and scores of doctors
to find buried in the stunned body.

Scars are the past trying to
take the shape of our flesh.

Your wife bares a breast to feed your son
and that's a wonder,
how love transforms bodies.

Are women the more natural
vessels for love?

Women have never been alone.
Men, too, are changed,
though our stubborn flesh denies it.

~

You plan to raise your son
in the love of words. Line by line
he'll grow more human.

These lines, as scarred as either of us,
mean to say the work

goes on. It does whether they say it
or not. I trust
the same can be said of you.

It's late. Anything more I'd say
would be an effect

of the hour, not the heart. Goodnight,
friend. Pray all our wounds heal.

Birds

for Charles Simic

My brother's throat was often swollen.
An illness, our mother said.

But I knew his habit of swallowing birds,
having watched him stalk. Sparrows
mainly, never any bird that was black.

My brother liked to say his throat
was dark enough. He would

hold a bird, his long fingers curved
around the warm feathers,
open his mouth wide, raise it as a chalice

and slide it down his throat,
the song of the bird going down
a dim, unrecognizable chamber music.

My brother's throat would swell for days.
When he started to talk of crows,

saying they were the only bird worth
swallowing, no one knew but me.

~

I remember how my throat seemed so small
and empty as they lowered
my brother. And the birds, all the birds.

An Egret in Flight

The promise of water birds brought us here,
the migration on
and this, we'd been told,

a place they come to, moved by calls
that can't be ignored.

The morning marsh wind surprises us.
Cold, we embrace.

Canada geese come in over us
to land in shallow water,
their ease in the air a revelation.

Through binoculars, the marsh comes alive
with birds my wife names from a book.

I say the names, and the air of my saying
means nothing to the birds,

the naming meant to convince us
we belong here
where the egrets ignore us

~

until we get too close and one startles
from the water, its wings
left over from before any fall or grace.

Weightless

The boy opens the withered heart, believing
it holds the dead. His father has

shown him the hearts along the back fence
and spoken of scattering the spirits

on the wind, how, at the moment of release,
you can make a wish. He wishes

the dead might make it to heaven
and runs wind through them. They do

a vague dance then fly, but won't let go
of the earth, clinging to the grass,

his clothes, and furring the screen door
his father stands behind. A lie,

the boy believes, must be white and weightless.
What the heart bleeds won't wash off for days.

The Weight of a Foot on Grass

Too young for the bar, the boy taps the glass
from outside, his father holding the bottle
as though it's a woman, or maybe what he lost

in a field near Pechong, Korea, his friend
finding too late what they were
looking for, clearing safe distances for others.

Heading home, they come to a field
where light calls everything
into question. His father drops to his knees.

Behind him, the boy curses everything
he can't know, what keeps him
from saving his father, from knowing why

he needs to trust the earth and the ghosts
buried deep enough they won't explode
with the weight of a foot on grass.

Tonight, in a dream, my father relaxes
on his lawn. Wind
jiggles colored lights strung on wires.

~

Everyone he has loved has come to this
backyard party. Barefoot,
my father drinks warm beer and laughs

with a man in uniform. Behind them,
streetlamps converge in the distance
under the grotesque limbs of oaks

crossed like the ribs of boats
that enclose this quiet
suburban street like a cathedral.

Carbon Cycle

Carbon haunts us. Ashes to ashes. The dead
placed years below lie down in us.

Not like the dead carved above ground.
Call that nostalgia.
The dead hurt us less long dead,

soil a distance, a lie, like the ash
on foreheads on a Wednesday

near the end of winter. Nothing living
rises from the smudge we mark ourselves with
to eat of the body and feel blessed.

We call the act of love a consummation.
Perhaps the world is consumed,
sex a revenge on the cold earth

for accepting flesh. Take. Eat. This
is my body given you for the sin
you can't pray your way out of. The body

can consume itself. We call it cancer,
the carbon-black intrusion in the light of bones
projected blue-white on a wall.

~

We try to exhume the ash and pray
the scars heal clean. Grief,
a dark lozenge we slip under our tongues,

tastes of cinders. Bitter, it reminds us
wounds bring the body to mind.

For the Workers of Machinists' Union, Local 765

And work is before us in grime,
and in erosion, and in rust.
No wonder we're too busy to rejoice,
unless work is rejoicing.
—William Matthews

They wanted to be anonymous as the metal parts
I lifted into columns toward the massive ceiling,
or the steel dust I shoveled from their machines.

They spoke the sweat and dust of their lives,
repeating stories as if they were foreigners
struggling with a new tongue. They spoke of

wives and I lusted for women I'd never met,
wanting to understand the broken passion
of their language under the humming lights

that never went out. The few night shifters
gathered round the clock when I punched out
spoke the same language. At home,

my parents yelled at one another the pain
they knew as love. Those men said life is
enclosed by suffering, steel dust in our mouths

~

no worse than the aftertaste of any labor.
Once, a water pipe burst over us. Told to leave,
we danced instead. Wet, we closed our eyes,

threw back our heads to drink, then went back
to work. Those men, working,
shared all they could in the stifling heat

and the dust. They had few words for
the life away from work they joked about,
but knew without it they'd die of the work

that, if allowed, could become all they knew.
My brother drove a forklift in the yards and left
after his finger was severed. He was lucky.

Someone wrapped it and sent it with him
in the ambulance. He quit, deciding
the risk wasn't worth it. Now, his finger works

as if nothing ever happened and he works
a safer job. It's hard to see the scar.
But it's there, the ragged signature of risk.

The last time I drove by the plant, I'd worked for
years to teach their kids. *Risk*, I told them.
Only then can you learn what you need to know.

~

It was quitting time for what had been my shift.
They came out the massive doors
and headed for cars, laughing and slapping backs.

They knew where they were going, and that
the work would go on without them. I wanted to
get out and go slap their backs and tell them

the stories I had learned since leaving. More than
the security fence stopped me. The work
that had made me one of them was in the past.

All I could do was try to remember how to
speak the love that keeps them sane.
Left without the work, I have to use words

to make it real enough to know they go on,
working on what comes to them as though
it matters, as though what they do can last.

How Breath Escapes Us

A half-naked woman dove into
this pool in December.
Her outline's gone. It's April,

a girl poised for the first dive
of the season.
She doesn't know her body

echoes the arc a woman is
forgetting under the earth.
The shock of the water

wakes her body. We need
to deny how breath
escapes us like steam, how

we can love the dead
even halfway,
like Persephone. Or

an almost naked woman diving
into an icy pool
as if that could settle

~

anything. To chalk the shape
of her body, they had
to break through ice and snow

before drawing the position
she was found in,
frozen, fetal. Like

the empty space in the body
of a new mother,
everything settling back into place.

One Form Love Takes

for Jordan Douglas Smith

You come out of water
as dark as the sea
your grandfather disappeared in

twenty years before. By going on
we celebrate loss.
Like your father, working

two winters in northwest Ohio,
where weather's memory,
to write what he needed to

release from his flesh. Since
it's April, even
where your grandfather went under

with 33 others from *The Liberty*,
celebrations are
coming to a close

for the story of one man's love
going on
beyond the loss of his body.

~

Pale flowers picked days before
are dying. Sometimes,
loss names us. Your father

wrote of a cold, mournful sea,
and love breathing
in gray water-light. He holds you

and pronounces your name,
the myth he means
to shape your life. You are

one form love takes, born
into a history of loss.
It's April 22, 1987, and you cry

at the sudden and stark light
that's all you know
of the world. We lie, say

loss doesn't belong here.
Believe the lie
and reach for your mother's

bare breast. Take the sea
within you, warm
with what will become memory.

The Reassurance of Soil

We count the broken bodies beside roads,
casualties. Collapsed,
they remind us things go their own way.

Some places they're kept from quick rot
by heat and a lack of moisture.

In this county, rains come often,
the bodies lost to run-off within a week.

In bars, we talk of what's coming. Later
we curl into lovers,
seeds coiled tight in the dark.

We don't forget the true lyric's about life,
not death. We don't need
elegies, our names in stubborn stone enough.

It's weather we'd outlast, not time. Still,
it's not stones we discuss over last call.

In mirrors, we've seen the bodies we pass over
break for the side of the road, as if

the spirit refuses, as long as it can, to give in
to the body's knowledge of brokenness.

~

Even drunk, we smell the soil in the air
we come out to at closing, our breath
ghosting us and the collapsing moon.

Renditions of Men

Abandoned barns fill with animals
they weren't built to hold
that come and go through ruined walls.

Some fields lie fallow, the bitter ruin
of corn brittle and plowed under.

In winter, every field the same blank
brilliance, children, raw
from the cold, build renditions of men

in stark landscapes. A pale moon rises,
a rumor of something
solid and far off. Snow covers

everything but a few ragged stalks
of corn. The shadow of

an owl hunting things small enough
to carry off breaks the spell.

Where it dives, the snow's disturbed,
stained with a struggle,
the white, subtle bones of motion.

The Unspeakable

Moist wind off the lake
can lift us
out of any sense

of direction. Gulls drift between
signs of life
in an overcast sky.

Those of us at home wait
for rain, the light
unbelievable. Imagine air

with the tone of a black and white
TV screen at night,
the breath of someone asleep

in the next room. There's no drama
not human, yet
this sky, laden with

its clouded light, seems tragic.
The rain's a relief,
letting everyone share

~

what unspeakable light soaks
the world. I imagine
rain touching windows,

fogged-over, streaked,
you speaking
with people who are mysteries

when you're here with me,
when we ask
one another to please

pass one thing or another
and furtive glances
of flesh force us to

imagine distances. Today the sky
is more important
than anything I can't find

words for. A single gull
sails the wind
and this loved world

shivers with a grief-stricken light
so absolute
it could stun

any one of us who happened
to look up
from our work.

Navigation Without Numbers

Things exist and change in time.
—Wynn Bullock

We come back to light when we need everything
certain. What we see is the past,
an illusion, formed by the right fluids,

where it's easy to believe the child dreams
of moisture, that he can't see

the lines we need to navigate by
and wants to slip back, without a splash,
into the water under the skin of the woman

collapsed under her own drought
by the bed. Codified in this exposure,
she's lost hope in any course mapped out.

Birds cross a thin horizon, the light that seeps in
where flesh joins flesh to form the dark.
The birds are sleep. And the woman is

crying, seeing, in the dark air, the feathers
of birds her father used to shoot,

~

laughing like a child. We can't see any birds,
only fledgling shadows in the rafters.

The woman would touch the child
but is afraid of getting lost
in the motion, of misjudging distance.

She has no numbers to guide her, no lines
she's sure of anymore. She hums,
but we can't hear light, and the dark

waits to consume everything. Without
numbers to count with, the child doesn't
know time passes. The woman knows

there's nothing to count on, not even the child.
She might reach out to hold him
and pass through him and hear a rustling

in the trees as though something had been
scared off. She might,
in moving, lose her sense of position.

She's afraid everything is held together
by the calm assurance of a moment,

that even a naked woman reaching for her child
might rip the lines tied to the silence
that contains everything in this picture.

~

Asleep, the child follows birds that follow
what they believe are necessary lines

and feels the feathers that will drift through him
all his life. The woman has lost sight of

the lines, and wants to feel the feathers.
Nothing moves. The lines, unused,

grow brittle. From our perspective
outside of light, there is no motion.

The woman accepts the pretense and leaves
her child on the bed, waiting for this
shell to tremble and break open from inside.

A Sad Ballad Haunted by Coffee

Coffee's not responsible for shadows
in landscapes as dark as the ballads
a man listens to up late with whiskey,

his loved ones asleep. I've cursed
coffee for keeping me up
after a woman woke me whispering

words risen from her sleep and regret
to stain me the way coffee stained
my shirts the aching mornings I kissed her

awake, the taste of coffee never enough.
Coffee kept me going. All night, trains
sounded more human than her sleep-language.

What can be brought to us or carried off
along tracks we drive over, slowing
enough to avoid spilling the coffee in our laps?

I want a train to cut through this town
and carry the dark words of a woman
to a man who can put them to music

~

and sing them with just enough pain
to laugh. I want a whiskey bottle
empty on the table, coffee brewing

in the stark light of the kitchen
where a woman who doesn't talk or curse
in her sleep is pouring two cups.

The Worst We Can Do

No one would put me in a poem, he said.
Waiters in French cafés are everywhere,
but not me. We were sharing a last drink

in a Midwest bar. He could've been
anyone's father but mine.
I always knew when my father got home.

The door would slam. No matter how
drunk, he never forgot to lock it.
Nights he got home early, he'd fall asleep

half-naked in front of the TV which droned
until my mother got out of bed
to turn it off. Sometimes she left him

there, limp in his wrinkled clothes.
Other nights she'd say his name
until he got up and followed her to bed.

It hurt her, and I couldn't understand how
she could limp through such pain
and still love him. But she did.

~

And the man who would pour me a free one
at the end of the night, who was not
my father, told me, *A good woman is*

what this place needs. We finished our drinks
and went home. I wish I had
told him love makes it through the worst

we can do to it, but I didn't see that till now.
And by now it would do him no good.
Either it would be old news, or unbelievable.

White Explosions

Sometimes what we say
rises perfect and means nothing,

unable to remind us of our pain
as we go from work
home and back to work,

like the insects we lit candles for
the summer evenings
we'd sit out for cool air

with beer and whatever needed to be
talked out. We killed bugs

despite the sweet-stinking candle,
and watched yards go dark

until we were alone under stars we knew
by name. Then, grief exploded
like a myth in our living rooms.

We waited weeks to see the wreckage,
and spoke of how things strike water.

You mentioned *The Fall of Icarus*,
and said everything had changed.

~

We spoke of the need to look away
and the other need

to watch, over and over, in slow motion
while the last voice said things
insignificant in light of what followed.

I see white explosions in the sky,
you said. Time will come,

you said, when grief will be white
and steady and rising on smoke,

or graphic, its remains laid out
to walk through and photograph,
no words left to describe it.

Fallen from Grace

They're set out late October, as though the dead
could want such bodies to come back in.

The dead will have nothing to do
with these awkward bundles of old clothes
propped up and stuffed on porches.

Air down from Canada sifts the garden
my wife's been working in

to harvest the last of the squash
and turn the soil for the winter.

A wood trellis leans sullen on the garage,
the beans that had climbed it sealed in jars.

Some bodies hang limp from ropes.
Street lamps shadow the drift down of leaves,
the wind's voice parched. My wife

shifts beside me, the sheet that ghosts her
mimicking the wind. Outside,
a body thrown together rolls over wet grass.

~

Fog settles. By morning it will be soaked.
My wife will remove the shrouds
from peppers and the mint she'll use on lamb.

Sambaine, she'll say, is a time for gathering
and saving what we can.
The dead won't come back. Tonight,

lights in kitchens and living rooms cast shadows
of bodies over the grass,
their elongated forms misshapen, familiar.

The moon, rising, dims them. Knowing
what nights these are, we carve faces

in hollowed-out squash and try not to think of
the bodies, or the cold we know is coming.

What Brings Us to Ourselves

This courtyard of coarse brick comforts you
from the wind. Blood thinned with gin,

you could be Tiresias returned to the dead,
the sense bought from his voice by sacrifice

dissipated. The dead don't want things to be
what they are. Say this courtyard's walls

are cliffs. Far back in caves warmed by fires,
Lakota dream your pain is the pain of gods.

Loss, they say, nests in our hearts and bears
ravenous young. I remember a Lakota who drank

to forget. With enough gin, all that mattered
was legend. He stood on one scarred leg

and worked his thick arms until we knew
he could fly. A woman touched him,

wanting to share the grace. She couldn't see it
was grief, what brings us to ourselves.

Tonight, the wind given voice, your pain
wakes us to sore bodies longing for sleep.

~

Your words could be Indian, or Greek.
Our bodies, gray at windows, could be ghosts.

Brought to this by your grief, we listen
without knowing why, until one of us

tells you to shut up and go sleep it off.
The rest of us join our voices to his,

a Chorus urging you gone, as though
this chant could give us back our lives.

Storms We Can't Name

Storms are days coming and never leave,
sticking around in local stories.

Like the one my father told of an ancestor
who drank too much and died
drenched to the skin. The storm

that took him comes back each spring,
a reminder who to blame
for joints that ache with drops in pressure.

I work these fields as long as weather
lets me. When storms come,

I tie things down and take my wife
to bed. Nights I enter her,

I believe I'm at rest in the eye of a storm
I can't know the name of. Later,

our bodies calm, I watch her sleep,
her breasts lifting and falling
to the anonymous rhythm of the wind

that sends me in to touch a woman
whose flesh holds its violence, and its calm.

With Bread to Fill the Air

Rain again. My wife wants to listen
with the lights out. This means
we can't make the lake, she says.

Or afford the faith it would take to
leap naked over a fire we'd built

on the darkest day of the year and believe
we called back the sun.

Days we do make the lake, gulls are hungry
and circle, assuming
we've come with bread to fill the air.

Across the courtyard a light comes on,
disrupting the dark. Imagine,

my wife says, hillsides lit up
in winter with prayers set
by men and women to call back the sun.

There's an island nearby we like
to visit, walking slow,
trying to name the voices of birds,

~

warblers singing. All of human history
hasn't made anything better.

My wife sings to sparrows, and laughs
on bridges barn swallows nest under.
They skim water without touching the surface.

We can't help but love their certainty.
My wife, made unsure by weather,
sings in Welsh. It goes well with the rain.

It could be a song about fires on hillsides
where families chanted prayers
they'd been taught, believing

what they did made a difference. Maybe
it did. Sometimes I'm not sure

how real something needs to be
before it's believable.

My wife wants to know if the lake's possible
tonight, after the rain. I think

of the surface, marked with rough weather.
Yes, I want to tell her. I tell her *Yes*.

Acceptable Damage

The sky a wound past the edges of buildings,
my wife and I burn blue-white,

storms off Lake Michigan elaborate gestures
we love to watch, though
we know the damage they could do.

Iron rods on roofs out west rise into skies
too open for the calm reason of percentages.

Faith hangs on where metal steeples tower
over towns, the black marks of collection
an accounting of those who've been saved.

Count the seconds, my wife says. We wait
for sound to tell us how far this light's come.

Thunder disturbs the air. *That was close*, she says,
her whole body burning blue-white again.

We've seen storms move in over prairie,
the twisted antennas repaired by men, unsure

on the raw geography of roofs, who
couldn't afford to pay someone to fix things.

~

I've learned to fix some things, but nothing
as grand as antennas that listen
in their rarified country to tell us

what we want or need to know. Nothing
that could be hurt by the sky
breaking into a blue-white wound.

I fix things we touch every day and depend on
but never praise. My wife and I,
naked in bed, watch the sky fragment again.

It's farther away, she says. I want it to go calm
before it reaches any place it could scar.

I want there to be no damage a man can't fix.
The way, sometimes, a simple touch can heal.

Acts of Erasure and Acceptance

There's no reason my wife should believe
how the light of this storm
folds into the backyard walnut trees.

Maybe she doesn't want to see what light does
to this world she's denying herself.

She talks of a woman who took off
into lush desert, her body
found, dried out, days later.

Her footprints were not, she says, frantic
periods, but calm ellipses.

It's difficult to go on from here,
to remember she's in
the lobby of a clinic in the Southwest,

surrounded by women who seem no more
than excuses for suffering.

I want her body to hold more, to believe
the light they pass over her
can turn back enough darkness.

~

The storm has broken here. No light
left to speak of. She reads
stories from the local paper. Tonight

it's about a man in Minnesota
whose son didn't call
on Father's Day. She reads of the blood

washed off walls in the son's house,
the bodies carried out, and wishes
they had interviewed the father.

She wants to know what it's like
to kill someone so close.

I want to ask if she can imagine
what it's like to be so forgotten,
but can't be sure how she'd answer.

The dark cells in her body are quieter,
she says. She feels better,
but says no when I ask to visit.

She's not ready. She folds out
the paper, another story.
I want to erase them all. Just one

more, she says, and reads of
a man in a wheelchair
who saved a baby from drowning

~

in a backyard pool. It's almost enough
to make me believe the dark
is dying inside her. A black branch

has broken and fallen against our home,
scraping brick as wind gives it life.

There's so much I want to say.
Where she is the stars are
out in unselfish numbers. Across

the damp courtyard, a light comes on.
It's good to know this world
isn't empty, that people are

coming together in rooms full of light.
A man and woman are forgetting
why they yelled this morning.

He's inside her and she's urging him on.
By morning this may be forgotten,
but tonight, for someone, being together

is a celebration, and enough. I want
to call back, tell her I want her home,

despite the storm. I want to live with
the hard evidence of her going.

Local Anesthesia

If it's just a question of knowing facts,
go back to the house where you knew the wind

and the woman you slept with
mumbled words you couldn't make out.

Ice illuminates the walks and edges of buildings,
like it did the night the man who knew
everyone's first name died in the snow.

You want to believe you could bring him home,
alive, and salvage your past.

The way you want loss to be something solid
in your flesh the local GP could locate

and cut out in his office, making small talk
as he operates, asking after your wife.

You want to believe it's possible to come home
bandaged and find her there and ask
what it was she dreamed when she mumbled.

She'd say nothing and touch your face,
her hand colder than you remember it
ever having been, cold enough to burn.

~

The pain wakes you back to a world
unaltered by memory.

While you're back, visit the stone you bought
and had cut with his name,
the same as yours. After learning

words can't cut the stone closer to meaning
than it already is,
your car is warm when you get back in

and starts right up, though frost has formed
on the glass in place of your breath.

When you pull into the drive, it's clear the house
hasn't been lived in for years.
No one but you has come back to visit.

Clouds are moving in fast and the radio is
talking blizzard. You would stay
but for the storm you see building.

The house would not keep you from the cold.
You pull onto the highway.

Behind you, the front hits. Everything
goes white, the light
it becomes more than you can stand.

Trusting Your Way Home

The radio picks up a song by Dylan
about slow trains coming.

They can be heard long before their smoke
rises, a hunger on the horizon,
steel laments punctuating parched fields.

After work, your father would drink for hours
where men gathered to discuss the lives
they worked to keep free of doubt and debt.

Don't doubt yourself, they said,
when you came to help him home.

The fields he worked are backyards now,
most of the tracks gone to weed.

Children play with rusted spikes and chant
things you'd recognize,
residue of the town you lived in.

Everything you believed would last
has changed. Still, your wife
sees you in the landscape. It happens.

~

We mistake strangers for loved ones.
The way you did once,
passing a town, the fields luminescent

in your headlights. You could have
turned down the street
where the house you grew up in

fell in on itself, and the odors of soil
and your father's body
would have welcomed you home.

But you drove on past those fields,
the few lights on late in town heartless.

Now, sun reflecting off spikes, you're home,
and nothing's what you expected.

Things are missing. The tree whose roots
you marked with words you meant to keep
private has been ripped out and burned.

There's been no rain for months.
Yards should be dead grass
and clothes discarded in the heat.

Not this green, everywhere the growth
of watered, well-tended blades.

People come out to welcome you home.
Your son laughs in your wife's lap.
Suddenly everything's easy to believe.

~

You've only been gone a day and are glad
you didn't lose your sense of direction.

Getting out of the car, you wave to
your father, pleasantly drunk on the porch.

A long whistle clarifies the distance,
and everything you could've lost
comes back, even the chant you carved

into one of the roots that etch
your backyard, a map you know by heart.

Open Between Us

We said little not suggested by the map
kept open between us. You knew stories
of places I'd never heard of. When you didn't,

we made up local histories and lied
about legends. We made love in
every state we passed through. Near towns

that showed on the map, you turned the radio on
for human voices. We kept to state routes
to avoid traffic and cut through towns

we didn't see a soul in, this country emptier
than I knew. You were quick to point to
the signs of people—house lights slanting over

flat land we both knew was too open. For
everyone who lived in the lit rooms,
the only salvation was the brief time of touch

after days of working on things they didn't get.
Like the man swallowed by the raised hood of
the same Ford pickup in every town. We came to

~

expect him and feel better when we saw him,
stripped to the waist and dark with engine grease.
We waved and in each town he waved back.

Sometimes a woman came out of a house in need
of a paint job to bring him a sweating can
of beer. In some towns, there was only the house

and the need. Sometimes, a child would be
in the cab pretending to drive. Other times,
no one around for miles, we wanted to stop

and have a beer with him, say how good it was
to see him again, how worried we were
about him being alone. He'd have talked of men

he knew by their first names who welcomed him
at the local tavern, men intimate with
the hard taste of wind who had taken home

the ruin of their lives when they were younger
and less tired. We're tired, too,
you'd have said. He'd have looked us over

and laughed. Stay out here long enough,
he'd have said, and you will be. I would have
thanked him for the beer, and we'd have climbed

back into our truck and driven as far as we could
before stopping to make love in a different state
no matter how tired we were. In the next town,

~

the Ford would've been by the road, the hood
raised as if he'd just gone inside. You would
have said he wasn't alone, that he'd gone in

to hold a woman whose lips were full of
local color that could pull us out of the stories
we made up to pass the time between towns

close enough to send the music that led us
to this northern city where the air
is wet and failure has signs other than dust.

Against all good sense, I want to go back to
one of the towns he was alone in
and invite him to the tavern for a drink.

He'd open up, admit his failures, and everything
lost to the stubborn silence of
the wrecked engine would be recovered.

We'd know each other by our first names,
which would be the same, and after
a long afternoon of pool and drinking

we'd step out and, light-stunned, not be able
to say which of us should stay in town
and which should start the drive back to you.

~

We wouldn't care who stayed and who left,
only that whoever stayed would be able to
make the engine in that Ford turn over.

George Looney's previous books include the tenth annual White Pine Press Poetry Award winner *The Precarious Rhetoric of Angels* (2005), *Attendant Ghosts* (2000), the 1995 Bluestem Award winner *Animals Housed in the Pleasure of Flesh*, and the award-winning novella *Hymn of Ash* (2008). He is Professor of English and Creative Writing and Chair of the BFA in Creative Writing program at Penn State Erie, The Behrend College, Editor-in-Chief of the international literary journal *Lake Effect*, Translation Editor of *Mid-American Review*, and Co-Director of The Chautauqua Writers' Festival.

Breinigsville, PA USA
08 June 2010
239420BV00002B/2/P

9 781934 99